REAL ROBOTS

by Grace Maccarone, Nancy Krulik,
and Jolie Epstein

Scholastic Inc.
New York Toronto London Auckland Sydney

To Bernice,
a real human being!

Acknowledgements

The authors would like to thank Dr. James Crowley, Jerome Hamlin,
Walt Disney Productions, and Eva Moore for their kind assistance.

Cover Illustration: Sandra Shap
Photo Research: Elnora Bode

Photo credits: Dan McCoy/ Rainbow: 3, 9, 18 (courtesy of Carnegie-Mellon
University); Christopher Morris/Black Star: 4; © Lucasfilm Ltd. (LFL) 1983. All
rights reserved. Courtesy of Lucasfilm Ltd: 6; Faverty/Gamma Liaison
Agency: 13; © Walt Disney Productions. World rights reserved:16;
Phototake: 19; P. Plailly Cosmos/Phototake: 20 (top), 21; Diego Goldberg/
Sygma: 20 (bottom), 22, 23, 25; Prof. Michael Freeman: 26; NASA: 28, 29,
30, 31; CBS Toys/Ideal: 10; Tomy Toys: 11; Mary Jo Dowling/Carnegie-Mellon
University: 14.

ISBN 0-590-40266-8

12 11 10 9 8 7 6 5 4   9/8

Where are the real robots? They are in homes, in factories, in fun parks, and in space! They build cars, work with police, tell jokes, and play games. Ready or not, here they come!

You are having a party. The doorbell rings. When your friend comes inside, you are not the only one who greets him. Your home robot is right by your side!

"Greetings, Earthling! Nice to see you," says ComRo ToT, the robot.

Then ToT shakes hands!

After all your guests have arrived, ToT serves drinks to everyone!

Then ToT starts to tell jokes!

Your guests want to hear music, so you turn on ToT's built-in radio. ToT dances, too!

Believe it or not, ToT is a real robot!

A robot like ToT used to be something you saw only in movies or on television. Those movie robots are not real. They are just actors dressed up like robots.

R2D2 and C3P0 are the most famous make-believe robots around. They are in the <u>Star Wars</u> movies. The actors who played the robots are Kenny Baker and Anthony Daniels.

ow, there are all kinds of real robots that you can buy for your home. You won't find any people inside these real home robots. They have built-in computers instead. The computers let the robots move and talk all by themselves!

Hubot can say, "I love you." It can also say a thousand other words. You can play video games or watch television on its screen.

RB5X is a real pal. It can bring you flowers. It tells nursery rhymes, sings "On a Bicycle Built for Two," and plays a game called "Spin the Robot"!

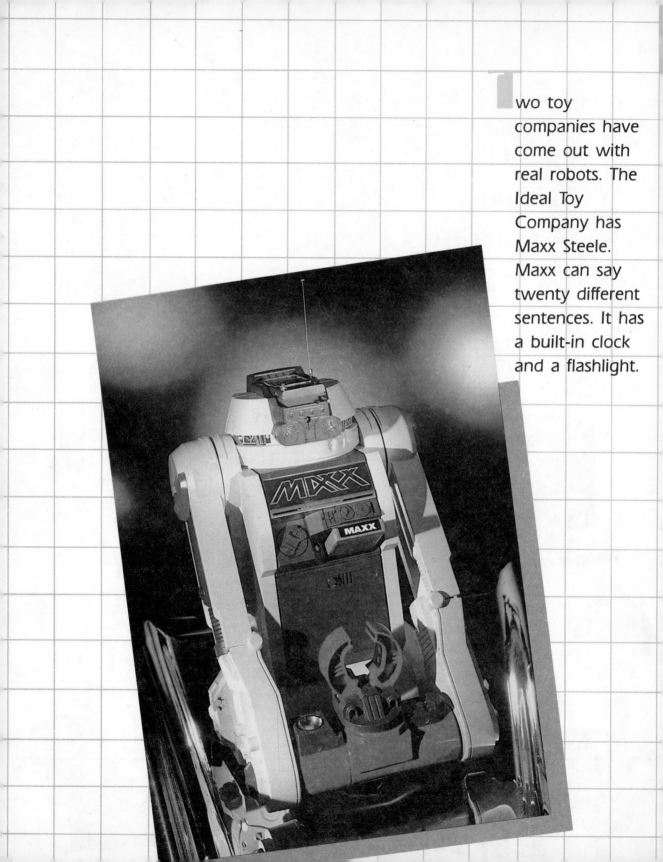

Two toy companies have come out with real robots. The Ideal Toy Company has Maxx Steele. Maxx can say twenty different sentences. It has a built-in clock and a flashlight.

The Tomy Toy Company has three robots: Ding-bot, Omni-bot, and Ver-bot.

Omni-bot can learn to wake you up in the morning. It can go to your bed and say, "Good morning." Then it can go to your brother or sister's bed.

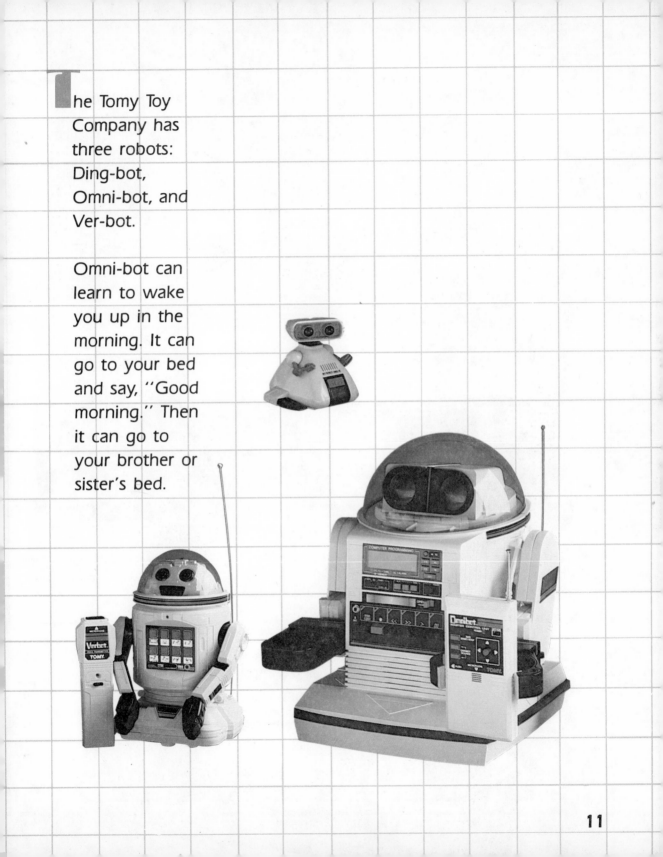

Hero 1 is a hobby robot. It comes in many pieces. You have to build it yourself. Then it becomes a home robot. It can see, move, speak, and lift things.

Hero 1's arm can lift things that weigh less than a pound. But don't count on it to go to the refrigerator and get you a snack. Hero 1 can't open the door by itself. And it can't tell an orange from a dog bone! You have to open the door and show Hero 1 where the orange is. You have to do more work than the robot!

Home robots are smart—but not that smart. They can't do the dishes, walk the dog, or clean up your room. Not yet, anyway!

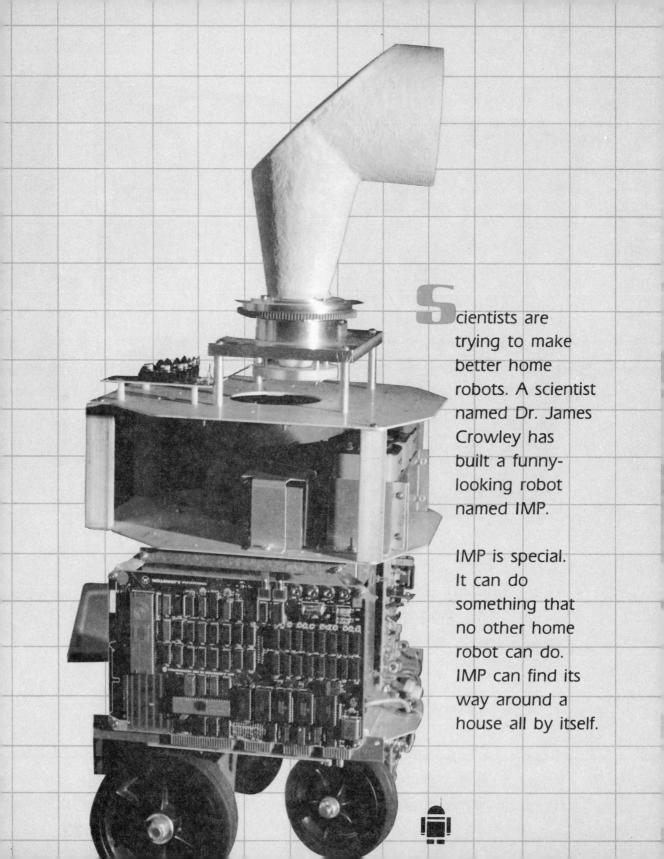

Scientists are trying to make better home robots. A scientist named Dr. James Crowley has built a funny-looking robot named IMP.

IMP is special. It can do something that no other home robot can do. IMP can find its way around a house all by itself.

Most home robots can only move around in one room, but not IMP! IMP moves all over the house.

IMP uses special robot sight to learn where all the chairs and tables are. It even learns the names of all the rooms.

Everything IMP learns is stored in its computer. Then IMP can go anywhere you tell it to — except upstairs!

IMP is also special because it can get around objects. Other robots get mixed up if something is in their way.

If IMP bumps into a shoe in the hallway, it won't get stuck like other home robots. IMP uses its computer and special sensors to decide how to get around the shoe. Even Dr. Crowley cannot be sure which way IMP will choose to move!

SMRT-1 (Smart-One) is part of
a new family of robots that is
learning to understand human talk.
You can see it—and talk to it—at
Walt Disney World.

SMRT-1 can understand two
words: yes and no. It plays games
to show how smart it is!

This is a number game SMRT-1 played. You can play along, too!

SMRT-1 said, "Let's play a game together. Pick a number from 1 to 10."

A girl in a Mickey Mouse shirt picked a number.

SMRT-1 asked, "Is it 1, 3, 5, or 8?" The girl talked to SMRT-1 through a phone. She answered, "No."

SMRT-1 asked, "Is it 2, 3, 6, or 9?" The girl answered, "Yes."

SMRT-1 asked, "Is it 4, 5, 6, or 10?" The girl answered, "Yes."

SMRT-1 asked, "How about 7, 8, 9, or 10?" The girl said, "No."

"I've got it!" said SMRT-1. Do you know what the number is? Turn the page to check your answer.

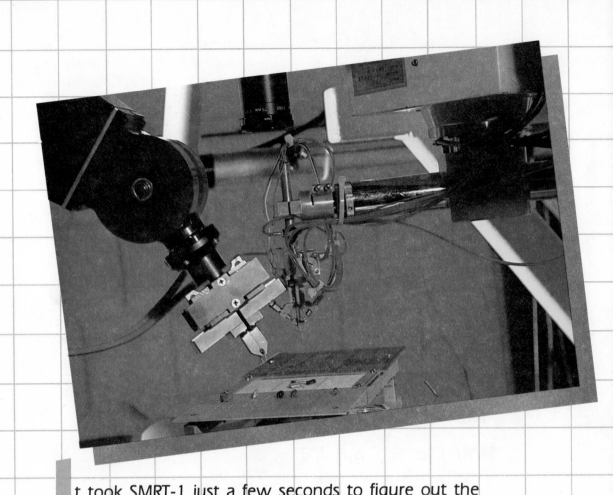

It took SMRT-1 just a few seconds to figure out the answer. The number was 6!

Working robots don't look as cute as home robots. But they get the job done!

Working robots are in factories, hospitals, police stations, and outer space.

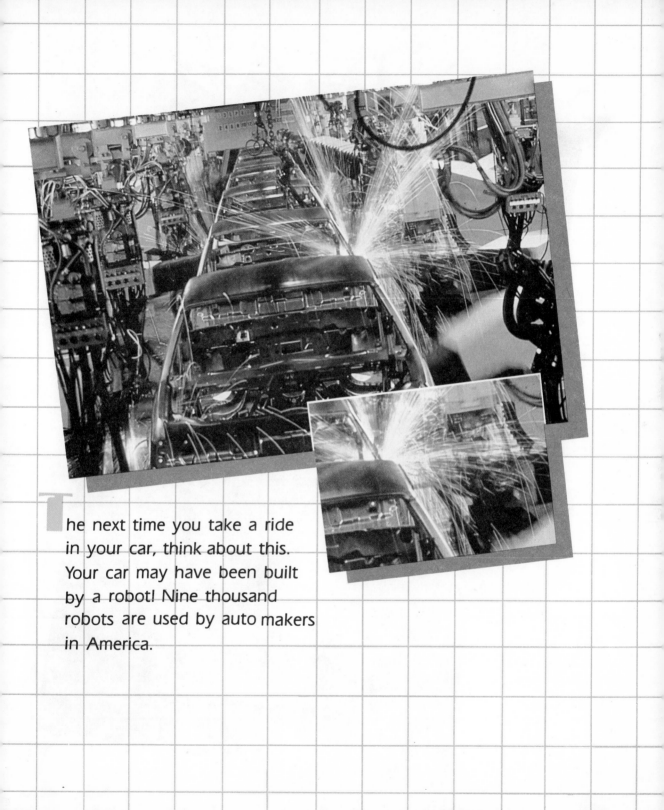

The next time you take a ride
in your car, think about this.
Your car may have been built
by a robot! Nine thousand
robots are used by auto makers
in America.

Robot painters do a smooth, even job.

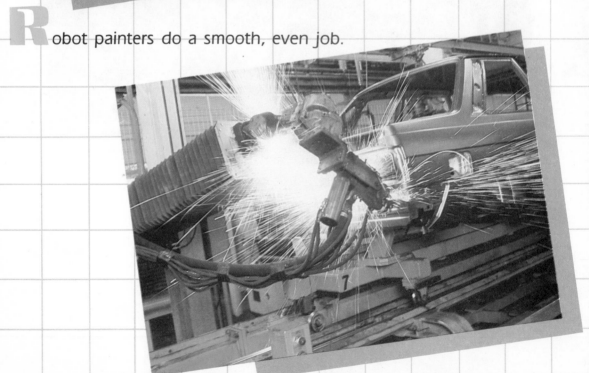

Robot welders join the different parts.

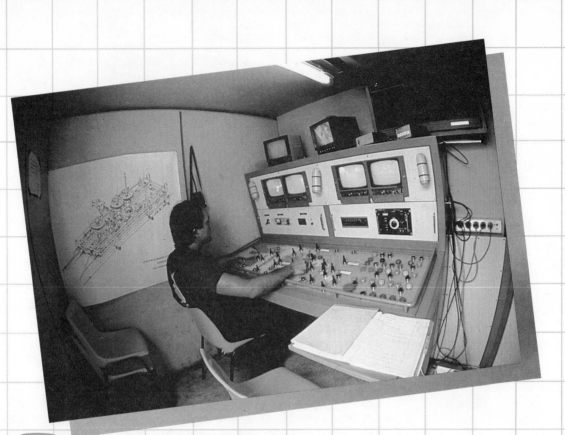

Of course, a human worker must make sure the robots don't make mistakes. He watches them on television screens.

Robots are good for some factory jobs. Robots never get bored. They don't get tired, so they can work long hours. And they can work in dangerous places with poisonous gases and chemicals.

RMT III is a member of the New York City Police Department's Bomb Squad. When there is a bomb in a building, RMT III goes right to work. The police stand way back. RMT III lifts the bomb and carries it to a special truck. Then the bomb is brought to a place where it can be taken apart.

RMT III saves police lives in other ways, too! If a policeman is shot, RMT III can pull him out of danger. RMT III is a real robot hero!

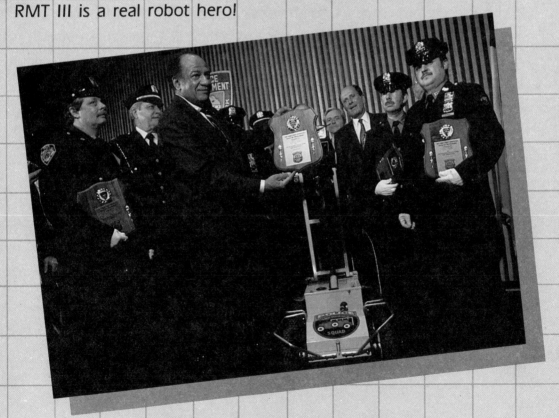

Some robots are built for people with special problems. There are seeing-eye robots that help blind people get around. There are even robot cars for people who can't drive regular cars.

It's not easy to make a machine that can do what a human arm or hand can do. Scientists are trying to make robots that can help people who can't use their own hands.

Some things that are easy for humans to do are difficult for robots. Squeezing mustard on a hot dog is one of them.

Wouldn't it be great to have a robot at school? Of course, it would.

The lucky kids at P.S. 107 in New York City did. Their teacher's husband built it for them.

The robot's name was Leachim. Leachim asked questions about math and science. If the students gave the right answer, Leachim told a joke!

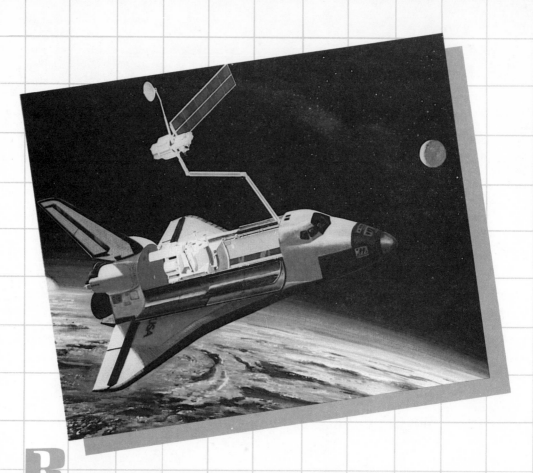

Robots seem to be everywhere. They are even in outer space. Lots of robots are out there right now.

The space shuttle has a robot arm. The robot arm can lift a satellite out of the shuttle and send it out to space.

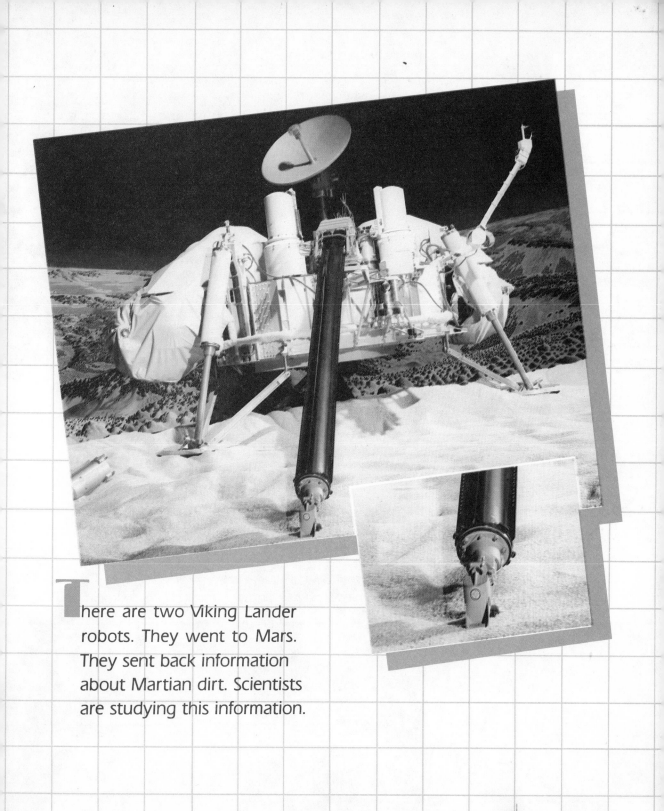

There are two Viking Lander robots. They went to Mars. They sent back information about Martian dirt. Scientists are studying this information.

Voyager I and Voyager II are also space robots. They have been to Jupiter and Saturn. They sent back information about the air and the weather. They also sent back pictures.

Voyager took this picture of Saturn.

Voyager took this picture of Jupiter (below) and four of its moons.

Voyager is traveling all the way to Uranus and Neptune. It will reach Neptune in 1989 and send back pictures.

Robots are really far out!